PRAISE FOR OTHER BOOKS BY PETER BURWASH

Improving the Landscape of Your Life

"Every once in a while, a really interesting read comes my way and strikes a chord. Peter Burwash has done just that. This is a man who really cares and who really wants to make a difference. And he does. His book is a blend of practical wisdom and depth of experience to teach us how to take charge in every aspect of our lives."

-Lee Iacocca

The Key to Great Leadership

"Inspirational and compelling bite-size quotes illustrated by motivational stories on two key competitive advantages of the future -service and leadership."

-Dr. Steven Covey,

Chairman of Covey Leadership Center and Author of The Seven Habits of Highly Effective People

"If something's not going right, The Key will impact your thinking on all elements of leadership. Its reminders are the ingredients of leading."

Tim

Total Health

"It's to your own good that you have picked up Total Health. Read it, and heed its wise and compassionate counsel, and you will be well on the way to a new level of aliveness, healing, and joy."

–from the foreword by John Robbins,
Author of Diet for a New America,
Founder of EarthSave International

"Peter again serves an ace with Total Health. He has been a role model for me for years and this book exceeds even my lofty expectations. No one can fail to benefit from time spent with Peter Burwash's approach to life, and Total Health is Peter."

-Howard F. Lyman, J.D.
President, International Vegetarian Union

"Mr. Burwash presents a collection of 'life lessons'... with the wisdom and compassion of a teacher who's 'been there'. This sage guidance on achieving Total Health is a gift - for your body, for your spirit, and for the health of the entire planet."

-Michael A. Klaper,
M.D. Director, Institute of Nutrition,
Education, and Research Author,
Vegan Nutrition, Pure & Simple

Becoming the Master of your D-A-S-H

Peter Burwash

TORCHLIGHT PUBLISHING INC.
BADGER, CA, USA
KOLKATA, WEST BENGAL, INDIA

Copyright © 2007 by Peter Burwash

All rights reserved. No part of this book may be reproduced, stored in a retrieval system, or transmitted in any form, by any means, including mechanical, electronic, photocopying, recording or otherwise, without prior written consent of the publisher.

Cover design by Kurma Rupa
Interior design by Kurma Rupa

Printed in India

Published simultaneously in the United States of America and Canada by Torchlight Publishing, Inc.

Library of Congress Cataloging-in-Publication Data
  Burwash, Peter.
   Master of your D-A-S-H / Peter Burwash

     p.   cm.
  ISBN-13: 978-0-9779785-4-0 (pbk.)
  ISBN-10: 0-9779785-4-0 (pbk.)
  1. Life. 2. Success. 3. Conduct of life. I. Title.
  BD431.B847 2007
       170'.44–dc22   2007000248

Attention Colleges, Universities, Corporations, Associations and Professional Organizations: Becomimg Master of Your Dash is available at special discounts for bulk purchases for fund-raising or educational use. Special books, booklets, or excerpts can be created to suit your specific needs

Torchlight Publishing, Inc.
For more information, contact the Publisher.
PO Box 52, Badger CA 93603
Email: torchlight@spiralcomm.net
www.torchlight.com

DEDICATION

This book is dedicated to all those wonderful people in uniform (military, police, and firemen) who make the sacrifice that allows many of us the freedom and opportunity to do something with our D-A-S-H.

ACKNOWLEDGMENTS

To Cie McMullin, who typed the transcript, to William Escalante, who did a wonderful job on the cover and interior design, to Sharon Digby for the painful job of editing, to Alister Taylor, my longtime publisher and special friend and to my family (wife Lynn, children Kim and Skyler) who afford me the tranquility to be able to put thoughts and feelings to paper.

CONTENTS

1. Develop an Attitude of Gratitude..................1

2. Stop Running Everydayathons....................16

3. An Ego Trip; a Journey to Nowhere...........29

4. Avoid Being the Richest Person in Your Cemetery................................36

5. The Best Things in Life Aren't Things......46

6. With Whom You Associate, You Become...56

7. Don't Knock the Shingles off Your Roof....67

8. The More You Fast, The Faster You Master the D-A-S-H...........................76

9. Plant Trees Under Whose Shade You do Not Plan to Sit......................84

10. Don't Let Yesterday Use Up Too Much of Today..................95

11. Life Never Goes in a Straight Line Nor Should It..................104

12. Never Forget to Look Up..................11

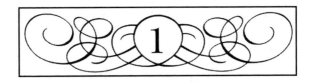

Develop an Attitude of Gratitude

Rare is the person that makes it through even one day without a challenge, a crisis, or heartache. In that sense, all 6.2 billion people on this planet have an equal opportunity. And that equal opportunity is how we deal with these bumps on the pathway of life.

It is amazing that you can have a day where 98% of it went right and 2% went wrong. Yet the 2% dominates your psyche. It is as if you were expecting a day with 100% good happenings every day. And the word expectation is one of your nemeses of the modern world. We must remember, though, that a day does not pass during which for even an instant we are in paradise.

> To know the road ahead, ask those who are coming back.

With the vast network of telecommunications available today, we have created a constant flood of desire—"Desire in the frontal crevices in peoples' brains everywhere." I remember many years ago being in a back street in a tiny village of China, and there were about ten people crammed into a tiny shack huddled around a TV set watching Robin Leach's "Lifestyles of the Rich and Famous." Here were these simple folk sitting shoulder to shoulder on wooden boxes on a concrete floor watching Robin's TV crew shoot panoramic views of the movie stars' mega-square foot mansion adorned in opulence, while the Chinese subtitles whistled by on the screen.

Develop an Attitude of Gratitude

That moment was one of the many times when I wished I could speak many languages, thereby allowing me to converse with these people in the shack. I would have loved to ask them what they were thinking. Could they see themselves in that situation someday—or were they scornful of all the wasted space and the ostentatious display?

Whatever the case, almost our entire day is one surrounded by overt or subtle messages trying to get us to want something. And so often, we fail to acknowledge what we have become because we are so concerned about what we want. We are truly in an affluent era. Eric Bloom's Economics class at Palo Alto Senior High School was an amazing example of this when they discussed some of the moral issues surrounding money. When the 35-year-old teacher asked his students to draw up a list of things they could not live without, most put pagers and cars near the top. Outside his class, the school parking lot is filled with BMWs and Porsches belonging to the students. The beat up Toyotas belong to the teachers.

The end result is a very frustrated global society. Enough is never enough. Wants once fulfilled give way endlessly to new ones. The rich want more; the average citizen wants more; and the poor want more. Hardly anyone understands that happiness does not increase significantly after one's basic requirements are met.

How often do you hear people genuinely say that they are "truly content"? How many of us ask God for something else, instead of humbly saying how appreciative we are for what we already have?

> No duty is more important than that of returning thanks.

Develop an Attitude of Gratitude

Even in our leadership role, whether it be as a parent, teacher, or manager, we have a propensity to expect more than we get. For those of you who are parents, do you recall asking your child to clean up their room? Reluctantly they trudge to their domain to execute this horrible task you have assigned them. They spend half an hour getting it nice and neat and clean, yet when you walk in you see an object on the floor. What is your first comment? "You forgot to pick up that pencil"—or hat or whatever.

The first thing out of your mouth is expectation—expectation that their room would be 100% clean instead of 98% clean. Why not recognize the 98% clean effort? Build confidence. Show appreciation. One hundred percent clean may come someday. (Note: Perfectionists have a higher number of mental and physical health problems.)

If you are fully conscious of this now, you will see how many times you do this in your role as a leader. Or, how many times your leader does it to you.

If you are going to be a master of your D-A-S-H, you need to begin with the basic premise you are going to live your life from day to day, without constantly expecting more. Instead, develop a core attitude of appreciating what comes your way, whether it is good or bad. The latter is more difficult to do, but it will be one of the major determining factors in mastering your D-A-S-H.

> Strawberries are too delicate to pick by machine... every strawberry you have ever eaten...every piece of this fruit...has been handpicked by calloused human hands.

Instead of a "why me" attitude, we can choose to respond with an understanding that life is a series of lessons. With each lesson comes an opportunity, and with each opportunity comes a learning experience.

We will face so many crises and challenges in our life, but none as tough as in a passing of a loved one. On March 6, 1998 I had a wonderful day at the beach in Hawaii with my two daughters. The sun radiantly reflected off the blue water as the palm trees swayed in the gentle breeze. The kids gleefully played in the sand and water. I sat in my comfortable beach chair reading. I paused periodically to make sure the kids were safe, and to reflect on the beauty of the day.

Upon returning home, my wife informed me that my mom had called from Toronto, saying that my dad was in a serious condition in the hospital, and the doctors didn't feel that he would make it through the night. With one fifteen-second sentence my heart had been rocked. I was 5,000 miles away, and my number one goal was to get to that hospital bed in time to say goodbye to my dad before he left his body.

As my wife and two daughters took me to the airport, my oldest daughter, Kimberly, said, "Daddy, you are crying." She had an idea of how much I loved my dad. She had got to know him and see what a great human being he was. But I could not expect her to fully grasp my emotions at this time. Right now, my focus was to arrive in time to say goodbye to the most wonderful man I have ever known. Not once, not ever, did he let me down. I had to be there for his transition.

I had written him a letter two months earlier and said everything I had wanted to say to him. Now I only wanted to be there to support him just as he had always done for me.

Develop an Attitude of Gratitude

For the past thirty plus years I have flown over a quarter of a million miles each year. Yet no flight had ever been longer than this one to Toronto. Throughout the flight I monitored his situation with calls to the hospital. He was still in a coma. I finally arrived in Toronto, and when I entered his room, there was my dad with my mom on one side and her friend Polly on the other. My mom said, "Peter is here." With that, he opened his eyes and said "Oh, Pete." And then we began talking.

We spent the next five days talking. I slept at the foot of his bed each night. On the sixth day it was time for him to go. With my mom on one side and with me on the other, we comforted him as he embarked on his final journey. I whispered to him, "Dad, I love you. Travel safely."

We all react differently to situations. My mom

was devastated. She had just said goodbye to her companion of sixty-two years. Yet, I was completely calm. I had cried openly and silently in his room for six days. But now there was peace around me.

They pulled the sheet over his body. My mom declined an autopsy, and I took her hand as we walked down that sterile hospital hallway. At it's end, there was a big blackboard with the names and the rooms of each person on the floor. I knew that "Mr. Burwash" would be erased shortly, but what he had done for me in my life was written in indelible ink on my heart.

I miss him every day. I think about him every day. I look at his picture every day. I thank him every day. I wish he could be physically here to watch my kids grow up. Yet, at no time from the moment he left, have I been depressed or not carried on with full service in mind. The reason is very simple: the key to a successful, happy life is always to appreciate and never to expect. This phrase has been permanently placed in the filing cabinet of my brain.

So when the time came for me to deal with my dad's departure, this is how I dealt with the situation and emotions, based on that very important phrase of appreciation versus expectation.

Fact 1: The plane flight felt excruciatingly long—yet it was only ten hours. If it had been a hundred years ago, it would have taken a month.

Fact 2: He had had cancer, yet he only really suffered for those six days in the hospital. I had so many friends whose loved ones had had long painful departures.

Fact 3: The doctor was incredibly insensitive and too busy to spend more than two to three minutes with him each day. Yet my mom and I were there—his complete family—one on each side for his final days in his body.

Fact 4: Though my schedule is usually very busy, when I got that dreaded call, I was free to be at my dad's bedside for his last six days.

Fact 5: I hardly ate or slept for those six days. Yet it was a wonderful feeling not to focus on my needs and instead, focus totally on the man who had served me faithfully all my life.

Fact 6: I felt bad that my mom was now without her constant companion of sixty-two years. Yet I appreciated how they maintained their friendship and marriage that long.

Develop an Attitude of Gratitude

Fact 7: He left us on Friday the 13th. It was a gloomy cold winter night, a superstitious date and an unappealing season. Yet, that night was a full moon, and my astrologer friends have told me that great souls travel when there is a full moon.

Fact 8: He was ninety-one years old when he left. I always thought he would celebrate his hundredth birthday someday. He had great genes. Yet I appreciated the fact I had had my dad for fifty-three years. A few days after the funeral I spoke with a good friend who had called. When I found out his dad had left him when my friend was only seven years old, I could better appreciate the long time together with my dad even more.

Fact 9: He outlived most of his friends, yet the pews were full for his service.

Fact 10: The hardest thing I ever did was the eulogy for my dad. Yet I was honored to be able to pay tribute to my hero. No matter how hard it was, it was the most important speech I have ever given.

Fact 11: I flew our eight-year-old daughter, Kimberly, to the funeral. Everybody said that an eight year old should not experience a funeral. Yet I kept a promise to her that she could come, and she ultimately participated in the service. I greatly appreciate how each night when I kiss her good night, she has a picture of Papa beside her bed.

It is always very easy to wallow in the mind-set of "why me" or complain about how life isn't fair. We can focus on the bad stuff, or we can focus on the good stuff. It is our choice.

Develop an Attitude of Gratitude

Nothing will ever completely fill the hole in my heart from my dad's departure. But most of the hole gets quickly filled up when I appreciate how lucky I was to have had a faithful, honest, humble, and committed dad, who so very much shaped who I am today.

Stop Running Every-day-athons

There is more to life than increasing its speed.
— Mohandas Gandhi

If you want to master your D-A-S-H, you need to take an inventory of your days. When most of you put your head on your pillow these days, you feel like your head has been in a washing machine, or your body has been drilled with a jackhammer all day. So many of you have insomnia, not because it is a disease or a health disorder, but because you can't wind down the nervous system and brain that fast. You don't stop a 150-mile-an-hour train in a couple of feet. Many of you lie down with your brain and body still in motion.

Stop Running Everydayathons

Many of you lie there and worry about what you didn't get done today along with what you have to get done tomorrow.

You spent the entire day functioning at mach-speed. You ate fast, drove fast, talked fast, answered emails fast, talked to your family and friends fast—and then suddenly you're in bed trying to slow down everything from your mind to your heartbeat. When you are on the freeway of life, it is not a bad idea to sometimes make a U-turn. Convenience has become today's love child. Fast food, faxes, cell phones, Internet—all these are supposed to make things more convenient and offer you a dream of having more time. Yet the majority of you have less free time.

Today we aren't working harder, just faster.

Previous generations worked very hard and had

long hours too. But when it was time for them to lie down at night, there wasn't this tremendous need for sleeping pills and tranquilizers as there is in today's society. This was due to the fact that most people had manual jobs. Their bodies were so tired at the end of the day that it was a pleasure to rest the body. Whereas, today many of you see sleep as an interference to all the things you have to get done or want to do. Your internal compass is spinning wildly.

Today most of you have overworked minds and under-worked bodies. You are living in a culture where most of you are cut off from your natural rhythms.

Speed has invaded your personal life. You are infatuated with speed, and while your speeding train is racing down the tracks, the scenery around you is a blur.

STOP RUNNING EVERYDAYATHONS

One of the unfortunate off-shoots of this rapidly paced environment you are in is that you feel an enormous sense of guilt if you step off the train and admire the countryside.

Early in life I realized the importance of a break or vacation. When we formed our company in 1975, I insisted that after one full year of employment, **EVERY INDIVIDUAL** working with our company was entitled to a one-month vacation. Whenever I mention to people that I am heading off to a tiny quiet island in the South Pacific for a month, almost every person says, "I could never do that. I would love to do it, but I couldn't be gone for that long." Do you know what their main reasons are? First of all, they are afraid of being replaced by someone while they are gone. And second, they feel they would lose clients or customers if they were gone that long.

I would like to address both these concerns. As far as your job not being there when you return, it is sad that our corporate world has created this mentality at all. Our corporate world is guilty, big-time, of a lack of loyalty. Unfortunately, loyalty seems to have gone out of style. The business sections of every paper are full of massive layoffs, firings, releases, etc. On the one hand, the companies want—and in many cases demand—your loyalty, yet in return they exhibit virtually no loyalty to you. Loyalty should be a two-way street in life and in business.

Today, leaders and many corporate managers bemoan the fact that employees are so mobile and that they will jump ship easily. Yet they don't realize that loyalty, first and foremost, begins with the person in charge. Study after study has confirmed that an extremely high percentage of employees (between 70 and 80%, depending on the study) leave their job because they don't like working for or with their immediate supervisor.

So if you combine the corporate philosophy of a lack of employee loyalty with poor leadership from the managers or supervisors, it is no wonder people have ten jobs in ten years on their resume.

A lack of loyalty means lack of trust. A lack of trust leads to worry—worry that if you take more than a week from your work, your position won't be there. So you take your laptop and Blackberry with you on vacation, check your email daily, and even though your body is on the beach or in the mountains, your mind is linked to your office and to your clients via telecommunications. That is not a vacation. Vacation comes from the Latin verb "to vacate," which means "to empty." You must empty your mind of that which occupies it most of the year.

And in fairness to your family, you should focus on them during your vacation. You read statistics that parents talk to their kids an average of fourteen minutes a day, or see that almost every person in prison says they hardly ever spent time with their parents. Why not take advantage of this opportunity to connect or reconnect? Remember, no matter what you have done for yourself, your company, or humanity, if you can't look back on having given affection and love to your family, what have you really accomplished?

As far as the second concern about losing clients goes, it is important to realize that a mark of a good leader is not what happens when you are there, but what happens when you aren't there.

Stop Running Everydayathons

A good leader trains people who can cover for you when you are sick or away. Admittedly, there will always be the occasional circumstance or individual that needs to be dealt with while on vacation. If you plan well and train well, you can vacate—vacate your job and truly have a vacation.

Because we have become a self-centered society, we don't spend enough time in other people's shoes. Let's start with your family. Think about the spouses who stays home and look after the kids. What chances do they have to "vacate"? When both spouses work, they arrive home to their children who have their own emotional needs and crave their time. When is there a break to wind down? Life is a nonstop treadmill of things to get done and people to take care of, and all of it has to get done, it seems, at an accelerated pace.

Master of the Dash

It is amazing when you study most people's calendars. They are crammed full of meetings, social functions, kids' activities, etc. There is no time for quiet time. There is no time blocked out for spiritual reflection. There is no time blocked out for self-realization.

If one visits smaller villages in India, the pathways and streets are full of people around 4:15 in the morning as they begin each day with their spiritual block of time intact. And it isn't just on Sundays—it is seven days a week. Simultaneously there is a tranquility and vibrancy on those village roads then. The hours before sunrise are always the best time for spiritual reflection, when a new day of hope is ahead of us.

If we don't nurture our spiritual side, we will drown in the ocean of materialism. Today it is even more important that we have a spiritual foundation as we are bombarded with hyper-commercialization. As you traverse through each day, you must be a strong spiritual navigator.

If the spiritual part of you is nurtured, you can face the frenetic pace much better. Just as loyalty has gone out of style, there is a segment of the population who shun spirituality as too "far out" or "off the wall."

Spiritualists are often looked upon as often being unrealistic. People who talk about peace and harmony, or faith and reincarnation, are countered by people who say what is important are the hard-core realities like shelter, food, water, and jobs. People today in the modern industrialized world will add spirituality to their day if there is time. Previous societies made it a foundation each and every day.

It isn't a coincidence that our focus on materialism has resulted in a proliferation of suicides, large percentages of people who are depressed, and a bored society that needs more and more stimulation.

If you want to master your D-A-S-H, you have to have a spiritual pillar in your life. We are spiritual beings. We aren't material beings. Except for our brain cells, all the cells in our bodies change every seven years. So every seven years we practically have a new body—materially. But spiritually we are eternal. We either improve our spirituality, or it regresses. But a major step in your life is first to recognize who you are. And once you do that, then you can begin to understand why you are here.

We are here to serve; this is what truly fuels us. If we serve ourselves, there is a limitation. If we serve others, there is unlimited capacity. If we develop a mind-set of serving others, then we can deal with our "everydayathons" in a much calmer manner.

Almost every one of you is talking about balancing your life. Books flood the market on the subject. You feel so out of balance for so many days. But the problem is you are talking about balancing your work life and your family life. These are all material pursuits.

What you need to do is balance your spiritual and material life. This is the real balancing act. While your material life may increase or decrease, your spiritual life must always increase. This allows you to be balanced. It will allow you to treat a material loss or gain with equanimity.

Everyone has spirituality. It is what gives your life meaning.

If you get a job promotion with higher pay, you have a choice of taking that extra income and buying "toys to play with," or you can use part of it to help people less fortunate than you. If you lose your job, you can see it as an opportunity to improve yourself. The biggest window for changing your self-concept opens when there is a failure in your life. Whatever happens to you materially, if you have a strong spiritual foundation, you will do fine. You will see the whole experience as a lesson, and your D-A-S-H will be that much better.

> My place in the universe is much more important than my place in any corporate world.
> — Mother Theresa

An Ego Trip—a Journey to Nowhere

In an ancient Eastern story, heaven and hell are exactly alike. Each is an enormous banquet where the most incredible, delectable dishes are placed on huge tables. Those who partake in the feast are given chopsticks five feet long. Here's the one difference. In the banquet in hell people give up struggling to feed themselves with these awkward utensils, and they remain ravenously unfulfilled. In heaven everyone selflessly feeds the person across the table.

A major step in becoming the master of your D-A-S-H is to stop being your own CNN. I am not sure exactly when it started, but sometime in the 1980's, there was a dramatic shift whereby the high profile individuals started to regularly beat their own drums. Perhaps it began with the sports world and the mass exposure it gets.

If God had made us to slap ourselves on the back, he would have made our arms longer. It is amazing to me today to see how many athletes are into self-celebration, particularly in team sports. Almost every time there is a score, a lot of other people did some incredible work. As John Wooden, the most successful basketball coach in the history of the game, stressed to his players, "Don't ever score without acknowledging your teammates."

Each year I do about one hundred speaking engagements, and I have been taking a poll from the audience as to how many people like the players showboating and dancing for the crowd

An Ego Trip—a Journey to Nowhere

after they have scored. Not one has put up their hand. NOT ONE. In fact many say how disgusting it is. Their showmanship and self-celebration just represents a lack of class. Playing professional sports today almost seems like a license for bad behavior.

The sad part is that the TV shows put these antics in their highlight package later in the day. And thus it is reinforced so kids can emulate their actions. Charles Barkley, former NBA player, made headlines when he said he didn't want to be a role model for anybody. Well, Charles is in a state of illusion. That is like saying Julia Roberts or Tom Cruise don't want anybody to recognize them when they walk down the street. Whenever you go in front of an audience, you are a role model. We are all role models—some good, some bad.

Unfortunately, many of today's athletes have shunned their responsibilities as role models in favor of blatant self-indulgence and disrespect for authority. Dale Robertson, in the *Houston Chronicle,* pandered his thoughts on professional basketball when he said, "The NBA is burdened by bad clubs full of post-adolescent millionaires covered in tattoos, projecting solemn attitudes, and playing uninteresting basketball in front of lots of grossly over-priced, often empty seats." When thoughtful intelligent people like Dale Robertson feel compelled to write something like this, then you know the pot of egoism has overflowed.

Even egotistical people don't like egotistical people. In the past, the egotistical person was in the minority on a professional sports team. Now they are in the majority. If you watch today's active athletes being interviewed on

An Ego Trip—a Journey to Nowhere

TV, it is amazing how self-indulgent they are in telling everybody how good they are. And what is the end result of constantly being their own PR agent? Ironically, they become even more insecure—because people are not attracted to this kind of behavior and they stop giving these self-centered individuals any compliments.

With this growth and insecurity, their life begins to spiral in the wrong direction. They either escape the real world with some addictions, or they commit a crime to get attention. Reading the sports pages these days is like reading a daily police report in a precinct. Instead of the Super Bowl or Orange Bowl, we will soon have the Jail Bowl.

And when they do get in trouble with the law, their defense lawyers argue that these are just kids and that their family life was a tough one.

Master of the Dash

Excuses. Excuses. This is the problem. People keep making excuses, and the end result is that you have insecure 35-year-old "adults" still trying to get attention.

> Fame contributes little, if anything, to our society.
> — Bill O'Reilly

Somewhere along the line, the younger the better, everybody needs to learn that they are not the center of the universe. That success and happiness is not based on how much you talk about yourself or sell yourself, but how much you do for others. Learn that it is more important to carve your name on people's hearts than on trophies.

If you want to master your D-A-S-H, here is a test for you.

An Ego Trip—a Journey to Nowhere

"I, me, my" fast for one day. Spend twenty-four hours without using these words. Some of you may have to begin with a one-hour fast. Regardless of the length, if you focus your communication, your attention, and your energy on others, you will see how differently people respond to you.

Good leaders, good teachers, good managers, and good parents all stress "we" instead of "I." The sooner you incorporate the "we" into your life the better things get—another notch in mastering your D-A-S-H.

Avoid Being the Richest Person in Your Cemetery

Every few seconds in the Western world someone dies of a heart attack, many at a very young age. And many had built up a very nice portfolio—a nice financial portfolio—not a nice health portfolio. Most sacrificed their health for their wealth.

> The poorest man would not part with health for money, but the richest man would gladly part with all his money for health. — Charles Colton

It is interesting now that there are approximately the same number of people that are eating too much as there are of people who can't get enough to eat. More people die today from the lifestyle diseases of heat attacks, cancer, blood pressure, osteoporosis, and obesity than from starvation.

If you are going to master your D-A-S-H, you have to have good health. If you are always sick or in pain, you are forced to focus on yourself, and you aren't much good to anyone.

Let's start with the most basic of principles, mainly the "fuel" for your body. Today, most people's fuel choices are driven by addiction. And there are no rest areas on the highway to addiction hell. I am not just referring to what we see as the standard addiction of drugs, alcohol, and cigarettes. I am also referring to our addiction to certain foods that have no place inside our bodies.

It is interesting to note that, left to a natural

environment, no living being will eat what they shouldn't in terms of how their body was constructed—except human beings. I would like to now address perhaps the most ignored or misunderstood statement of today's Western medical profession, and that is how little emphasis is placed on educating people about the importance of "gut transition time" (the time food stays in your intestines.) If more people understood this, they would significantly delay their trip to the cemetery.

Unfortunately today's medicine is based on the attempt to cure. This is what doctors get paid for. It is not financially lucrative to teach prevention. If people don't get sick, then doctors don't make money. Therefore, with the emphasis on cure, there is a strong resistance to focusing on why diseases occur, or prevention.

Avoid being the Richest Person in Your Cemetery

All the original medicines, from Ayurveda in India to many of the well-known Chinese disciplines, focus on the importance of prevention and the understanding of things like gut transit time.

Recently the Royal Academy of Physicians in Great Britain proclaimed that, "Ninety percent of all disease and discomfort is directly or indirectly related to an unclean colon (large intestine) due to impacted fecal matter." What a powerful endorsement for moving food through your body quickly.

To better explain this, let's look at our body's intestinal tract. Humans have a very large intestinal tract similar to all the vegetarian and fruitarian species. If we were meant to eat animal flesh (most are meat, chicken, fish, and eggs), we would have received a very short intestinal tract. In addition, we would have been given a set of tearing teeth and claws that could rip through a tough animal's hide within seconds.

What happens when you, as a human being, with a very long intestinal tract eat a piece of animal flesh? There is a long gut transit time. There are many ways of explaining the debilitating results of this, but the following can probably best illustrate it.

If you were to take a dead fish and put it on the road during a day with eighty-degree temperatures and return three or four hours later, the smell would be very unpleasant. Now imagine this same fish inside your body slowly winding its way through your long convoluted intestinal system in a 98.6-degree environment (your normal body temperature). The average time for flesh to make this trip in the human body is three to five days. Meat has zero fiber, and we don't have the acids like the carnivores (meat-eaters) to break down the tough sinewy tissues easily.

Having one bowel movement every two to three days is extremely unhealthy. A healthy person has at least one or two bowel movements PER DAY. The problem today is a majority of doctors only have a tiny fraction of nutritional knowledge locked away in a minute crevice of their brain. And their own lifestyles are such that they die about ten years earlier than people in other professions. They have only one bowel movement every two days, and they see that as normal. They pass that observation on to their patients. Well it may be normal, but it is not healthy. Your goal should be to leave nothing inside of you for more than a 24-hour period. This is why our creator gave lions, tigers, and dogs a short intestinal system—so they can move the rotting carcasses through their system quickly. Yet even at that, the number one killer of lions is parasites in their gut.

In humans, the majority of parasites are found in our colons. We provide the perfect environment for them to proliferate and grow by having compacted, slow-moving matter in our colons. They have a field day.

Here is an experiment for you if you currently eat meat, fish, chicken, or eggs. Continue eating these foods while studying your bowel movement for one week (the number, the color, the length, irregularity, etc). Then the next week eat grains, beans, nuts, fruits, and vegetables (a human being's natural diet) and see what happens. Within three to four days you will notice an increase in the number of bowel movements; the stool color will be lighter (indicating shorter

Avoid being the Richest Person in Your Cemetery

transit time), and they will be longer opposed to lumpier. It is not an easy or pleasant topic to discuss, but it is probably one of the most important things you can do to improve the quality of your life. Without regularly improving your health, you can't possibly master your D-A-S-H.

Here is another benefit: by changing what passes your lips, you will be contributing to the world around you. You will no longer be supporting violence. In the U.S. alone, nine billion animals are slaughtered every year to satisfy our taste buds. That is an incredible one million per hour. And it is a very violent industry. You will do your part to gradually decrease the continuing support of a more violent world.

Looking at it ecologically, our real home is the planet, and all species are interconnected. By not supporting the industry of the production of animal flesh, you will be doing the earth a big favor. Almost all of our land, air, and water are polluted these days. Less than one percent of our global supply of water is fresh and clean now. I have expounded upon this in the past, along with many others, on how damaging the meat industry is to our ecology (see my book *Total Health*). The rate of environmental destruction has reached warp speed in the last fifty years. Hung up on the human population surpassing six billion, we haven't paid any attention to the fact both the cattle and chicken industries have numbers exceeding these individually. And for what purpose? To satisfy a few inches of our tongue with the end result of numerous lifestyle ailments.

Traditionally, for millennia food intake was very simple. As people made more money, they added meats. And then along came more incidents of sickness. More people were making more money and thus spending more on things that were destructive to their bodies. As their financial stature grew, their health usually deteriorated. The childish dreams of overabundance must be replaced by more adult realities that limit the gobbling of resources.

Remember, your tombstone does not include your bank balance, nor does anyone erect a memorial in the graveyard or the mausoleum stating, "Here lieth the richest person in our ground." Make sure you leave something in this world besides clothes, a nice house, and a car.

The Best Things in Life Aren't Things
Don't Let Your Possessions Possess You

We have never owned so many "things." Houses have doubled in size in the last forty years to hold all this stuff; even our refrigerators have gotten bigger and bigger. The majority of households have more than one car, what to speak of TVs. Yet, on the crest of this wave of gathering more and more possessions, there is increased sadness. And with unprecedented stimulation around us, there is boredom. More people suffer from depression and other mental illnesses than any previous generation. We are at a cultural moment where noise and agitation are everywhere. Millions are drinking and smoking their lives away and watching television until they become mindless automatons totally controlled by illusory pleasures.

As we wade through this smorgasbord of modern life, what has caused this? First of all, we are advertised to death. In 1971 the average American encountered 560 advertising messages a day. By 1999 that had grown to 3,000 per day. People now buy more of what they want rather than what they need. We are bombarded with these commercial enticements. Life has become one constant upgrade parade. The end result is that we have become absorbed in sense gratification. And what is the basic message in most of these ads? They offer a better life for you. Your life would be more enjoyable if you buy it. You will be happier. You will enjoy life at a more intense plateau. These ads create desires that result in excessive sense gratification and attachment to the objects of our senses. When these desires are not fulfilled, people become frustrated and angry. One of the unfortunate results of this frustration is that people turn to crime. If people can't afford what they want, there is a propensity to steal rather than earn and save. If you get bored or unhappy, there are so many stimulants, both legal and illegal, that promise to change your mood and state of mind.

There are eight million people in prisons globally. Two million of those prisoners are in the United States, the land of "things" everywhere. We are now spending more money building prisons than we are putting up new educational institutions. And what's alarming is the increased violence with which crimes are being committed. Since the 1960's there has been a quintupling of violent crimes. Only the naive would argue this increased intensity of violence is not a direct result of the visual images flashed onto the eyeballs of today's moviegoers and TV viewers. I often wonder what it is that inspires TV and movie producers to put out so many violent, shoot-em-up, destructive-type images. I know the obvious is the lining of their wallets. But where is their responsibility? One has only to read the local or international news to see that we are living in a more violent world. Where robbers were once focused on petty theft with a flashlight, they now carry weapons to annihilate anyone in their path. Where rapists once committed just the act, they now often feel compelled also to kill that person.

And when they get caught, they immediately rush to get a defense lawyer who will argue what a horrible life their defendant has had, or they were temporarily insane. Nobody seems to want to go back and start to understand where all this negative energy and thought is coming from.

Master of the Dash

Children who are taught that all of life is precious, and who are made to feel precious themselves, do not feel compelled to commit acts of violence. We so often become what we see and hear. A perfect example occurred in the South Pacific island of Fiji when TV was first introduced to the country in the 1990s. Obviously, to support the new station, advertisers were needed. One of the advertisements was for the car jack. Car thefts in Fiji, until this time, were almost nil. Yet these ads showed how to break into a car and told people they really needed these car jacks to prevent future break-ins. Guess what? The Fijians now saw and learned how to break into cars, and car theft immediately went up. And car jacks were sold. And the advertisers were happy. And the TV station stayed in business. And crime continued to go up. And ultimately more prison space was needed.

The Best Things in Life Aren't Things

We have become a band-aid society. We gorge our bodies with the wrong foods and then plunk ourselves in a doctor's office or on a hospital bed and request as quick a fix as possible. We continue to produce violent images for people to see and then build more prison cells for those influenced by what they see. Instead of making an effort to get to the root of the problem, we seem content with a cover-up or a temporary plug in the dam.

> In my next life I want to come back as a poor peasant living within a third world country, where I am not plagued with materialism and notoriety.
>
> — Princess Diana

If you want to master your D-A-S-H, you have to become detached from the material "stuff" and develop a strong sense of awareness and self-discipline. Try to stop chasing the shadows of possession and power. The next time you go to the store ask yourself with each purchase, "Do I need it, or do I only want it?" Stop for a moment and look at the proliferation of worthless products staring at you from the store shelves.

Or take a day and go through your house and look at all the "things" you have that are not useful or don't have any sentimental value.

Moving can be a challenging yet wonderful experience. In 1999 we moved from Hawaii where I had lived for thirty years. We were moving to Carmel Valley, California and inquired about the cost of shipping items 2,500 miles across the ocean. We decided it wasn't worth the cost, so we increased the size of our moving sale to include almost everything. We did the traditional newspaper ads and posters on the wall. We priced everything very reasonably. And it paid off; between 8 a.m. and 1 p.m. on a Saturday, we

The Best Things in Life Aren't Things

watched 95% of our belongings go out the door. We kept only our necessary personal items, files, family memorabilia, and a few household items.

I can vividly remember the excitement and freedom. It wasn't from getting rid of everything or the fact I watched these possessions go out the door in just five hours, but rather that I wasn't attached to them. I was able to let almost everything go without a tinge of sadness or attachment. This is the way it will be when I have to leave my body—no material possessions will accompany me. This was a peaceful realization. Even when wealthy people are on their deathbed, their focus isn't on their BMWs, their Rolexes, the degrees they earned, or how much wealth they accumulated. Their focus is on family, friends, and their faith. This is ironic because if it were possible to build a thought meter and count the number of thoughts each day a rich person had about "things" or possessions, as opposed to friends, family, and faith, it would be the reverse. How much of their time was spent making money and shopping versus time spent on their spiritual growth? How many hours are spent in pursuit of a bigger financial portfolio than reading stories to their kids at night?

When I researched and wrote the book, *Dear Teenager,* I found there was a direct correlation between wealth and the time spent with one's children. The richer the family was, the less time the parents generally tended to spend with their children. The kids had lots of "toys" but were greatly deprived of love and attention. It isn't a chance statistic that the highest percentage of suicides among teenagers was in the middle to upper class income families.

A fellow I knew had just received a $1,500 check

from his dad, one of the many over the years. When he looked at the check, he had tears in his eyes as he said, "My dad doesn't understand. I don't want the money. Why can't he just go to the store and buy me a shirt? Then I would feel like he cared about me."

If you want to master your D-A-S-H, you have to completely understand that there are two ways to be rich. One is to have great wealth; the other is to have few wants.

> We should be content with what we have but never with what we are.
>
> We have multiplied our possessions but reduced our values.

With Whom You Associate, You Become

You learn something new every day if you pay attention.

There is a very good reason why parents are so careful about whom their children hang out with or whom they marry. Association is one of the most powerful influences of the direction your life will take. If you talk to almost any prisoner, you will find that the majority of their unacceptable acts of behavior were not initiated by themselves. In most cases they were encouraged, coerced, or pushed into doing something wrong by a peer, a friend, or a leader. Very few acts of ill-doing are solely the result of one person's thoughts and actions. Your friends and associates are like the

With Whom You Associate, You Become

button on an elevator. They will take you either up or down.

In assessing this step to master your D-A-S-H, take a look around you and see who you are surrounded by, wherever you are.

Over the years we have taken our tennis programs into many prisons. Behind these heavy gates and barbed wire are some of the nicest people I have ever met. They made some mistakes, but their core values are pretty solid. Even amidst people whose lives have taken a detour down the wrong path, there is good association. Even prisoners can seek out good association, or they can seek out those whose primary function is to escape or to commit more crimes once they get out.

Because our basic nature is to follow, we must be very careful who our leaders are. Whether it is a clique in high school, or in the workplace, or in your community, it is always wise to tread carefully before jumping into a group. It is nice to trust, but blind trust often gets us in trouble.

In the late 60s and early 70s, the hippie era ushered in a massive shift in the terrain of consciousness among the younger generation. The downside was a lot of wasted lives for those who fell into the dark well of addictive drugs. The upside was a major spiritual awakening—a revolt against the rapid materialistic trip of the post World War II era.

During this time of search for peace and happiness, along came a lot of gurus or spiritual masters, many from the East. The problem was that many of these so-called spiritual enlighteners were materialists under the guise of spiritual advancers. Many young people were searching,

With Whom You Associate, You Become

and in the process of choosing their "association," they neglected to do a little research. Basically, the process of seeking a spiritual guide or teacher should be no different from seeking out a life-long companion, a doctor, or a friend. In simple terms, do they walk their talk? When you really get to know people, there are a limited number who actually follow through on what they say. They say one thing and act otherwise. A true spiritual teacher or spiritual master is going to be exhibiting a purity of character at all times with no strings attached. Today you can go to any school (private or public) in the world and you will see two types of teachers. There is the category of the pure teacher who is doing it because it is their calling and they love it. And then there is the category of teachers who are just collecting a paycheck. The first group of teachers love teaching and they love learning from their students. Every person has had a teacher like that, and the impact they have on people is huge. Often, one teacher can turn a student's life around.

One of the reasons that politicians are so greatly distrusted is that they hardly ever follow through on their promises. And then the government wonders why voter turnout is so low. Periodically, there is a politician who really cares about serving the people and who isn't concerned with the power, prestige, popularity, and perks of the job. They deeply care. But their association isn't what they had anticipated. They are shocked about how the system works. They either become disillusioned and quit, or they allow the "association" to take over and dilute their values.

And in the business world, how many employees know that almost always top level management

With Whom You Associate, You Become

has a whole set of values that are different from the rest of the troops. They also see personality has replaced character as the prerequisite to success in their company. Our character is our destiny. There is no more essential aspect of any person. In any journey, our character will be tested. Who we become is a direct result of with whom we choose to walk down a path or with whom we choose to part ways. Always remember that character transcends private and public life (as former President Bill Clinton found out).

The choice is not always easy. An abused spouse might really be in love with her abuser. An employee may love his job but despise his dishonest manager. A teenager may feel great need for his circle of friends, but be in great discomfort when they pull out the drugs. An athlete may love his team but be deeply troubled by the coach's ethics. But our choices show who we are, far more than our talent or abilities.

The power of association is tremendous. This is why gangs, teens, cliques, and organizations become a significant force. The best way to determine if your association is worthwhile and one that can help you master your D-A-S-H is to determine what the ultimate purpose of that group really is.

If the purpose is to be of service to people with a significant positive direction, or if it is a process that will help build your character along the way, then you are probably on the right path. Your heart will most likely be the appropriate compass. It will feel right.

It was interesting interviewing gang members when I wrote *Dear Teenager*. Almost every mem-

With Whom You Associate, You Become

ber said they didn't feel right, but they were trapped—they couldn't leave because of fear of retaliation or ridicule.

Association of people, ultimately for a negative purpose, won't feel good whether it is a group or a pair. How many people have married someone for their money, fame, power, or beauty? The short term "glitz" was quickly overshadowed by the heart saying, "This isn't right." How many of you have said, "I should have listened to my heart instead of my brain or my hormones?"

A key component that you should look for in any association is harmony. And conversely, any union of people should have that as a prime priority. Where there is harmony, there is peace of mind.

I remember in the late 60s, playing the U.S.

Master of the Dash

Open Tennis Championships in New York. As was often the case, I had lost the first round, and doubles didn't start for another day. I wandered down to Tompkins Square, and there was a large group of people sitting on the ground chanting some songs. All around them was loud extraneous noise and a frenetic atmosphere. Sirens were blaring, drunks yelling, people arguing, individuals with scowls on their faces, all surrounded by massive amounts of concrete. Yet these people chanting and singing looked so blissful. They were totally oblivious to the chaos around them. They were in a pocket of harmony all together, all with smiles on their faces.

In life, we remember where we were when a major event happens, and we have a few powerful poignant images that stay with us throughout our lifetime. Those happy faces are still with me today. They showed me that association is ever so

With Whom You Associate, You Become

powerful. It helped me recognize this throughout my life. It elevated my consciousness. I was just an observer, not a physical participant, but I felt a part of the group's harmonious vibrations.

Recently, I was at a church rummage sale. It was organized by mostly female senior citizens. I realize why I like to go to these happenings. Sure, everyone loves a bargain, but what I like best about it is the association of the people and its purpose. You aren't going to get pressured into buying something by a high-commissioned sales person. The money that is spent will go to a good cause, not to support another person's lifestyle.

These women put their heads on the pillow that night knowing that during the day they associated with people whose principal cause was service—service without a paycheck. These people know that life is like a roll of toilet paper. The closer it gets to the end, the faster it goes, and time is limited for them to master their D-A-S-H.

> Be more concerned with your character than your reputation because your character is what you really are, while your reputation is merely what others think you are. — John Wooden

> A true friend or associate is someone who dances with you in the sunlight and walks beside you in the shadows.

Don't Knock the Shingles off Your Roof

There is often a fine line between someone who is confident and someone who is egotistical. If you want to master your D-A-S-H, you have to be confident that you are going in the right direction. Remember the feeling when you are driving in a car and are lost? You have no idea where you are. Well, the same applies in life. The only difference is that more people spend time looking at maps than they do thinking about the direction of their life. It is one of those things that seems to get stashed in the "to do later" file.

This is unfortunate because failing to learn what

our purpose in life is, is what causes people to kick the shingles off the roof. If you don't know where you are going or should go, then how can you be confident about this life?

There are two areas that are paramount when it comes time to be confident. One is your ability to perform certain tasks, and the other is knowledge.

If you ever watch a great athlete at the end of a game, they are the ones who are confident in their abilities to perform. Without confidence, there will always be doubt. And when we are doubtful, we tend to put ourselves down, either internally or externally. You have been around someone you just met and within five minutes they are telling you all their faults. It is as if they are at confession and feel compelled to unload. It is almost a cathartic exercise for these people.

From the beginning, their openness prevents you from finding fault with them later. At the opposite end of the spectrum is the egotistical person that we talked about in Chapter 3. It is important that you strive for a balance. You are confident about who you are and where you are going, but you don't feel compelled to tell people how great you are.

In order to have confidence, ability is good in sports, business, and the arts. But it is far more beneficial to be confident of your purpose in life and where you are going or progressing.

"Ambition without knowledge is like a boat on dry land."

With so many people today lacking self-esteem because of lack of confidence in themselves, there are a lot of vulnerable souls who are potentially very gullible. And for every vulnerable or gullible person, there are many more individuals who want to take advantage of these people. It's a tightrope walk for the seekers today. With such mass telecommunication capabilities, a person can learn about a lot of different paths. There is so much information available that at times it can be overwhelming to try to sift through the fast-buck fakes to find the bona fide teachers, scriptures, and philosophies. To compound this, we are often under the illusion this information is actual learning.

Yet the search is critical. Nobody gets in their car or a plane or boat or train day after day without knowing where they are going. Yet so many people take this trip called life and have not a clue where they are going. And then at a certain point in their life, they start questioning.

Don't Knock the Shingles off Your Roof

Sometimes one of the unfortunate turns in this searching process is that people rebel against their current situation without having an alternative path to follow. So much energy is spent in rebelling (kicking the shingles off their roof) that very little thought goes into its ramifications. And rebelling often leads to wars. Rebels tend to think they have a better way.

Look at religion. Religion, which was meant to be a bond of union, has become a source of sectarian strife. Instead of religion giving people a sense of confidence in where they are going or should go, it has brought two very negative feelings to the surface. First is fear. Look at how many people are killed every day around the world because they have a particular faith. So many atrocities are committed because an individual is of a particular religious denomination.

And second, religion can lead to arrogance when a person is so sure they have the "right way" that everybody who doesn't think like they do, or believe what they do, is destined for a horrible trip.

For those of you who are seeking, your challenge is to sift through the mind-boggling number of options you can take for your journey. But patient research pays big dividends for your spiritual path, and ultimately for your confidence in that path. If you reflect on your life so far, you will be able to recall many times when people tried to kick the shingles off your roof. However, if you didn't help them with the process, you are better off today.

When I was playing the junior tennis circuit, I got a letter from the president of our tennis association telling me to quit the game, as I didn't have a future. Instead of assisting him in destroying my confidence, I simply kept the letter and kept on practicing. And when I was in the finals of the National Championships many years later, I took out that letter as my opponent and I sat down during changeovers. I was ahead 6–1, 5–2, and instead of traditionally toweling off and drinking water, I chose to re-read this letter that had been written five years earlier. After ultimately winning the match and the championship, I had the greatest urge to go into the stands and say to this man, "Thanks for the motivation," but my dad and coaches had always stressed to win with dignity and humility.

You all have a similar story. But even more important, do you have stories (or an on-going saga) where you put yourself down regularly? You have little or no control over what others will say to deflate your confidence, but you do have control and can master the D-A-S-H regarding how you feel about yourself.

Over the years there are two denominators that separate confident, secure people from those who constantly belittle themselves. The first is that they have a very strong spiritual belief, and secondly they exemplify that spirituality without feeling superior. They do not make others feel inferior because they have another belief or because they have no belief.

A spiritual person has a deep well of compassion, both for others as well as themselves. They understand that they are here for lessons, and lessons involve mistakes. We will take wrong turns as we drive down the pathway of life, but our confidence in where we are headed allows us to have the courage and determination to return to the path. There are no shortcuts to any place worth going.

> Never believe you are better than anybody else but remember you are just as good as everybody else.
>
> — John Wooden's father

The More You Fast, The Faster You Master the D-A-S-H

If you study any religious scripture or doctrine, fasting is an integral part of the instructions for our lives. You can look at fasting in two completely different spectrums. One is that it is a sacrifice, a painful omission from something that you are greatly attached to. The other perspective is that fasting helps you with your self-discipline. And we can all use a dose of that.

In previous generations, involuntary fasting was something that was a part of almost everybody's life, simply because there were hard times.

The Faster You Master the D-A-S-H

People just couldn't afford things all the time. There weren't credit cards where people could plunk down a piece of plastic and worry later. Credit cards are one piece of the puzzle of instant gratification. We are now a society that wants things right away—no waiting. We have become so impulsive and present-oriented that we often become completely controlled by our own instant desires.

And with such an easy access to most things we want, we develop a series of addictions. In Sanskrit there is a word "goswami," which means master of the senses. When someone can master their senses, then they are able to make rapid progress on their spiritual path. Fasting has always been associated with spiritual awakening or enlightenment. Actually, if you look at it in very simple terms, your senses either control you or you control your senses.

For those who are controlled by their senses, they will have their temporary cravings fulfilled, but they take another step toward the cellar of addiction.

A great way to work on mastering your senses is to list all the things you cannot do without—coffee, soft drinks, drugs, ice cream, alcohol, meat, cigarettes, TV, talking about yourself, food, etc. After your list is complete, begin listing these addictions starting with the one you feel you are least addicted to or attached to, and finishing the list with the one you are most addicted to.

Then begin a 24-hour fast from one item. Some of you will have minimal problems with this; others will be in great anxiety.

When people fast they have two cravings.

The Faster You Master the D-A-S-H

One is mental and one may be physical. For example, for a person who says they can't start their day without a cup of coffee, there is the mental association with coffee and the start of a day. Then there is the physical craving, and if the craving isn't satisfied, then the body may begin to shake. If the latter happens, then you know your addiction has a strong foothold on you.

When I was younger (in my mid twenties), there was a time when I had a strong attraction for ice cream. I could eat a complete carton in one sitting. And that was daily. I wanted to see if this was an addiction. So I quit for six months. It was a wonderful feeling to know that is wasn't controlling me.

For new parents, a great opportunity to teach self-discipline is to do the following test. When your child is old enough to make some reasonable choices, put two plates out on the table. One plate has one cookie and the other plate has two cookies. Say to the child, "Do you want one cookie now or two cookies in one hour?" A few times of this and you will quickly see whether your child has an innate sense of self- discipline or not. Having a sense of self-discipline early will go a long way toward being able to fast as an adult.

Fasting is a powerful tool for advancing us along the road to self-discovery, conscious awareness, and spiritual transcendence. It allows us the peace that comes from being free of desire. And being free from desire is one of the cornerstones of mastering your D-A-S-H.

Fasting is also a cleansing time. When it comes to food, think about how few times in your life you have given your stomach a chance to rest. For many of you, your last fast was when you were sick. Your body said, "Stop."

The body is similar to your house. At some point you need to set aside all else and clean up the house. Our body needs that focus as well. Stop eating and let your body repair itself and clean itself up. The wonderful thing about our body is that it heals itself in most cases. Statistics consistently show that 80% of your health problems are cured without any intervention from your doctor. The moment you cut yourself or a foreign object enters your body, the body begins repairing itself.

The reason people's bodies finally break down and need significant medical intervention is almost always due to them constantly loading their mouths with something. There is no opportunity to do repairs, and the machine finally breaks down.

I mentioned that fasting is also a time for self-discovery. It is a chance to see whether your mind or your senses are controlling you. People who fast regularly get a strong sense of accomplishment and confidence. It is very difficult to feel good about yourself when you know that things are controlling you.

How often have you said, "I know I shouldn't have this desert, but…" It's nine at night, your stomach is beyond full, but your sweet tooth is doing battle now with your brain. The phrase, "A moment on the lips, a lifetime on the hips," is just one part of the equation. The biggest part is whether or not you can say no. If you do say no, you will learn that that sweet craving disappears in ten to fifteen minutes anyway, and by saying no you will once again have conquered your senses.

Fasting is not deprivation. It is a positive step forward in your endeavor to stop thinking about yourself so much. It is a mega-step in mastering your D-A-S-H.

"If you live in harmony with yourself, you are apt to live in harmony with others."

Plant Trees Under Whose Shade You Do Not Plan to Sit

"A person is grown up not when he can take care of himself, but when he can take care of others."

There is an old Chinese proverb that says if you want to be happy for one hour, take a nap. If you want to be happy for one day, go for a walk in the mountains. If you want to be happy for one month, get married. And if you want to be happy forever, serve others.

Many, many people who have overcome addictions not only love the freedom, but they also spoke of how inward control of the senses resulted in an outward service approach towards others. Once you stop making yourself the center of the day, you are free to help other people. And if you want to keep mastering your D-A-S-H, you have to see service to others as a major step forward.

As I was writing this book, I was also doing media interviews on my previous book *Dear Teenager*. Although there are many popular topics to discuss relevant to teenagers these days, every interview included a discussion on teenage suicide. With teenage suicide skyrocketing in the western world, it is of great concern particularly for parents of teenagers.

While there is rarely only one answer to any problem, particularly one with such inherent complexity, I do feel strongly that there are two very positive directions one can take to help prevent suicide tendencies. If you look at most suicide notes, there are usually numerous references to "I," "I can't go on," "I can no longer cope," "I have had enough." In other words the prime focus in suicide cases is on that individual thinking mostly of himself or herself. The person who commits suicide is very selfish. And selfishness is born out of a lack of an environment where a person is taught to concentrate on others. People who spend most of their time in service to others don't think about suicide for two reasons. First, they are enjoying the happiness that comes from their service, and second, they just don't have time.

Why is it that such a high percentage of suicides are committed by middle to upper class teenagers? They have so much materially, but aren't satisfied with their multitude of possessions.

This leads us to the second suggestion for people who are contemplating suicide: simplify your life. The more you have, the more frustrated you get because these "things" aren't bringing you the happiness you thought they would. And this frustration is often what starts people down the path of suicide.

> When it is dark enough, you can see the stars.
> — Ralph Waldo Emerson

If every child could learn this early in life, I feel confident that the suicides would go down dramatically. If you take a teenager to an old folk's home for a few days of service, they will see life in a different perspective. They will get to see a lot of older folks who are reluctant to move on. They will hear them talk about how they wished their lives hadn't gone so fast or how much they will miss their family.

Or take teenagers to a children's hospital and visit the hospital floors where kids are terminally ill with cancer. Or maybe a trip to a poor section of a foreign country might help bring things into perspective. Almost every person who develops a service attitude talks about how much better they feel about themselves when they make others feel good. However, if you want to master your D-A-S-H, this should not be a reason for your service. The best service is one that comes from your heart without any expectation for reward or accolade. Your intention should be your reward.

A by-product of serving others is exemplified in the famous study by David McClelland. He found that simply showing a group of subjects a documentary film about the work of Mother Theresa strengthened the subjects' immune systems.

Plant Trees Under Whose Shade...

Once people start focusing on a "paycheck" for service rendered, something is lost. You can always feel it when a person is serving you because it is truly in their heart or whether it is just in the interest of their receiving their paycheck. This is why I feel it is very important to start children out with the understanding of service without a reward or "allowance." They can get an allowance later on for other situations, but learning to help out because you want to, not because you have to, is a significant step toward building a good D-A-S-H.

One of the reasons people feel so good about volunteering is that there isn't an exchange of money attached to the endeavor. However, in today's society there tends to sometimes be suspicion attached to volunteering. Suspicion as to why you are doing it. In Hawaii many years ago, we took our tennis program into the state prison. While the program was met with a lot of enthusiasm, there was also a lot of suspicion among the prisoners as to what our motives were. They wanted to know how much we were getting paid. They wanted to know what we wanted from them. These were guys who had very little trust in anything most of their lives. They couldn't trust their parents, their friends, their families, or society, so they wanted to know why we would take a chunk of our time to come in and teach them tennis.

We told them that the real reason was that when we started our company, we all sat around on the floor one night and decided which segments of the population we could bring tennis to on a complimentary basis. Each of us had written into our contracts that we were to spend a minimum of two hours each week donating our time to the community. So we chose people in wheelchairs,

Plant Trees Under Whose Shade...

the blind, the deaf, the mentally challenged, and prisoners as recipients of our time and teaching.

It was only after we kept doing it week after week that prisoners saw that the gift we were giving them was from our hearts. They really got into it when one of our professionals, Bruce Haase, helped them build a new tennis court. What was even more amazing was, as the prisoners in our tennis program got released from prison, the first place they would come was to our office. They said that they felt closer to us than to their families. We went into the prison for eighteen years every week (except for the occasional shutdown when there was an internal problem). Even the church minister didn't make it in each week. We became a rock for them, one of the only things in life that they enjoyed and that they could count on. And the only reason we had to stop was that the crime rate in Hawaii had accelerated so much that they needed more space for more inmates and our tennis court gave way to more prison cells.

Over the years we won many awards for our special programs. It was nice to be recognized, but it was all very secondary to the immense sense of satisfaction we got. When I am asked in media interviews what has been the highlight of my coaching career, without doubt the two that stand out are my seven years of volunteering to play for the U.S. troops in Vietnam and the prison program. At no time in my teaching career was I ever so much appreciated as by the prisoners. They always met me with an enthusiastic smile and were fully focused during the time I was in there. And every one of our professionals who went in there felt the same way.

Years later I called one of the prisoners at his

workplace and left my name and number. He told me that when he saw my name on the phone slip he started to cry. He said that during his darkest moments in life, we were there for him like a bright star. He appreciated the fact that when he got on his furlough, we would go to the beach and just talk.

When we first set out to take tennis into the prisons, it wasn't a planned out effort. In fact we literally didn't know if we would be around the second week.

In the beginning there was apprehension as we first entered the prison in our spanking clean white shirts and shorts. We got our share of catcalls. But over time we gained their trust and respect. The catcalls turned into excitement. We became what they called "the highlight of their week."

We definitely went in there to plant a tree without planning on sitting under it. That's for sure. But for all of us, students and tennis professionals, it became a symbol of friendship that transcended those heavy iron gates. We all felt good about our D-A-S-H.

Don't Let Yesterday Use Up Too Much of Today

There is no question that memories are a second chance for happiness.

Almost everybody loves to reminisce. It is why the "Oldie Stations" on the radio are so popular, or why people like to look at photo albums or watch old movies. There have always been references to "the good old days."

People have a natural inclination to throw out the bad stuff of those days and focus on the positive experiences of their past.

A good example of this is a mother who fondly looks back on her child falling asleep in her arms as one of the most peaceful feelings in the world. That dominates her memory of her baby's life. Filed in the deepest recesses of her brain are the innumerable smelly diaper changes, the sleepless nights where she robotically got up for feedings, and her increasing fatigue from her seven-days-a-week, 24-hour-a-day "job." Years later when picking up her grandchild or another young baby, all the positive flood of good memories would race back, and a smile would come to her face. It is said that upon birth a chemical, Oxycitin, is released in our brain that makes us forget our nine months in the womb. Otherwise we would have nightmares about being suspended upside down in a tiny enclosed area surrounded by smelly organs. And in many ways, after birth, time is that "chemical" that tends to wash away the heartaches and difficulties that many people had.

On the other hand, there are people for whom the opposite occurs, whereby they cling so tenaciously to the unpleasant experiences of life that they can't function. Day after day they carry the heavy baggage of life's valleys. It prevents them from carrying on a normal life. Rare is the person who hasn't had some personal tragedy to deal with. And as the daily news reports the turmoil that ravages many parts of the globe, people can easily be disheartened.

We all bring certain fears or phobias into this world. When I was three years old, I was terrified to cross any bridge. I remember being on my tricycle with my dad and coming to a bridge. The overwhelming fear of crossing the bridge that day is still in my mind today. Another phobia I have is being in the ocean with my feet dangling under water. I am convinced that there are sharks everywhere wanting to have my feet for dinner. Where did I get these phobias?

It wasn't until I read Dr. Weiss' book titled *Many Lives, Many Masters* that I understood this. He documented hundreds of cases of people under hypnosis who he took through their past lives to find out where their real problems lay. Since I had always felt we were on a journey of many lives (and many lessons), I now know that my fear of bridges came from another life, since I had never fallen off anything high in this lifetime.

What is important in our life is that we not allow our past, whether in this life or past lives, to inhibit us from mastering our D-A-S-H.

The adage "we are certain of only two things

in life—death and taxes," is not true. Some countries don't have taxes, and some people in the world will never pay taxes. So the only real certainty for the six billion plus inhabitants of this world is death.

But do we really die, or does just the body die? A majority of people feel (or have faith) that the body dies and we live. In fact, if you have ever witnessed a person die, the people around him are crying, "He's gone." The body is still there. In our hearts, most of us know we move on.

And most people believe that there will be a reward or punishment during the transition or departure from the body. In the Christian faith, it is heaven or hell. In the Hindu faith, you get a type of body according to your consciousness at the time of death. In some Buddhist doctrines, you will go into a void.

Master of the Dash

Whatever the case, we will probably be going on a trip. And this is where the past can play a major role in where we go. But the key is to extract certain things from our past to help us master our D-A-S-H so we can prepare for our trip. We all have things we have done that we aren't anxious to have anybody know about, or things we did out of ignorance. I am not one to hold regrets, but rather prefer to learn from these lessons, and not wallow in my misjudgments.

In 1970 I had been convinced by a group of doctors that my athletic performance would be dramatically enhanced by becoming a vegetarian. As a staunch carnivore who preferred steaks cooked fifteen seconds on each side, this was not music to my ears. But my two years at pre-medical school had allowed me to understand the reasoning, and I had agreed it would be a good idea to try it. Not doing very well on the professional tennis circuit at the time, I needed every advantage I could get.

In order to reinforce my new lifestyle, I decided to visit a slaughterhouse, hoping that the experience would be distasteful enough to discourage any of my potential future cravings for meat.

I was totally unprepared for what I saw. No words in our language can describe what I saw. The sights of the slaughterhouse are forever etched in my mind's eye.

It was a hellish environment: screams, horror in the eyes of the animals, blood, intestines, eyeballs on the floor, and mean, non-smiling workers. But do you know what emotion I had? It was one of complete shock. How could I have been so ignorant of how that neat cellophane package of red meat made it to the grocery store? This was such a powerful experience that I have never even once contemplated supporting that industry again. If forced into a choice, I would starve first. That is how much it impacted my life.

Although my heart ached and went out to these poor helpless creatures, the upside of all this was that the experience laid an even stronger foundation for my values and morals.

If you want to master your D-A-S-H, you have to be an expert filter. Do not be upset with your mistakes, but learn from the lessons that they taught you. If people have hurt you or offended you, either forgive them or forget them. But don't let them continue to enter your consciousness and create a revengeful mentality.

Don't Let Yesterday Use Up Too Much of Today

The West has taught us an "eye for an eye and a tooth for a tooth" mentality. Mahatma Gandhi said, "An eye for an eye makes the whole world blind." If you continue to hang on to negative experiences, your life will be miserable. The people of India and the Middle East understand this point much more than most Westerners. In India they believe in the law of karma (action/reaction)—whatever happens to you, good or bad, is God's grace, so they accept it without being revengeful. In the Middle East you hear "Enshahla" a lot. It means, with Gods will, whatever happens—good or bad—is His will. In other words, stop trying to be the controller of the universe. Keep serving. Keep learning from the past. The door to the past has been physically shut and the key thrown away. So any trips inside your rooms of the past should be for the sole purpose of mastering your D-A-S-H—today.

Life Never Goes in a Straight Line—Nor Should It

Remember that not getting what you want is sometimes a wonderful stroke of luck.

— The Dalai Lama

A man found the cocoon of a butterfly. One day a small opening appeared. He sat and watched the butterfly for several hours as it struggled to force its body through that little hole. Then it seemed to stop making any progress. It had appeared as if it had got as far as it could and it could go no further. So the man decided to help the butterfly. He took a pair of scissors and snipped off the remaining bit of the cocoon.

Life Never Goes in a Straight Line

The butterfly then emerged easily, but it had a swollen body and small-shriveled wings. The man continued to watch the butterfly because he expected that, at any moment, the wings would enlarge and expand to be able to support the body, which would contract in time. Neither happened!

In fact, the butterfly spent the rest of its life crawling around with a swollen body and shriveled wings. It never was able to fly. What the man did not understand was the restricting cocoon and the struggle required for the butterfly to get through the tiny opening is God's way of forcing fluid from the body of the butterfly into its wings so it would be ready for flight once it achieved its freedom from the cocoon. Sometimes struggles are exactly what we need in our life. If God allowed us to go through our life without any obstacles, it would cripple us. We would not be

Master of the Dash

as strong as what we could have been, and we could never fly.

To a novice gardener, a lot of rain early in the season may seem like a blessing. But a seasoned farmer disagrees, because if the weather is too easy on the plants, then the crops may only grow roots on the surface. If that happens, a storm can easily destroy the crops. However, if things are not easy in the beginning, then the plants will grow strong and roots will grow deep, seeking out water and nourishment below. This way they are much more likely to survive a storm or a drought.

So it goes with your life. If things are too easy for you in the beginning, you almost never develop the character to dig down deep into your well of perseverance, or the will to get through the tough times.

Life Never Goes in a Straight Line

In many ways it is a plus not to be talented in an endeavor that you want to pursue. Why? Because talented people don't have to work as hard to develop the necessary skills. The result is that there is a tendency to take it easy because things have come so naturally.

Take an athlete who is highly talented. In the majority of cases they don't practice as long or as hard as the less talented. This is unfortunate because later in life they will have deprived themselves of the tremendous learning experience called "struggle." However, if this talented athlete is fortunate to get a great coach, then he will be much better off. Bill Walton, a Hall of Fame basketball player, said that when he was at UCLA, his coach, John Wooden, made them practice skills and drills over and over again and each time a little faster. He said when it came time to play the

Master of the Dash

actual game, everything had seemed in slow motion.

> Winning is great, but I prefer the process.
> — Arthur Ashe

Distance runners who have trained well say the same thing about a race. Those who have struggled in the practice arena love the actual race because they have prepared well. And life is no different. If you talk to successful people, they started preparation at a young age. They had innumerable challenges and mountains to climb. Life wasn't a straight line for them, and they are better off for it. Then there are the people who say competition is bad for you. They don't want kids competing. This is so sad for the kids' future because they will eventually stumble out into the bright lights of the real world and see there is winning and losing in all aspects of

Life Never Goes in a Straight Line

life. Everybody has to learn to win and lose along with the process of the struggle.

In the beginning days of golf, golf balls had smooth covers. Then somebody discovered that the ball would go further if it was roughed up. Thus began the manufacturing of golf balls as we know them today, with dimpled covers. So the analogy to life is that it definitely takes some rough spots to make you go furthest.

Earlier we talked about the critical importance of health. Yet we continue to buy and use labor-saving devices that make things easier to do, yet contribute to our declining health. Think how many times you use the escalator instead of the stairs; or used things like an electric toothbrush, remote controls, automatic dialing—from small to big gadgets. We try to get away with minimal physical movement.

And the irony of it all is, by using these labor-saving devices, you will use up less calories. Gradually our bodies expand. And guess what?—most people today are carrying an extra twenty pounds or more than when they were teenagers. Imagine every day when you get out of bed, before your feet hit the floor, you have to strap onto your body a twenty-pound bag of cement. That is what the average overweight person is doing every day. Then is it any wonder why they regularly visit doctors and hospitals and pop pills to dull the pain in their overburdened joints? Have you ever watched people carrying something that is heavy? They can't walk in a straight line. Our lives today are full of shortcut options. We not only take shortcuts physically, but this also expands into our attitude.

There once was an elderly carpenter who was ready to retire. He told his employer-contractor of his plans to leave the house-building business and lead a more leisurely life with his wife, enjoying his extended family. He would miss the paycheck, but he needed to retire. They could get by.

The contractor was sorry to see his good worker go and asked if he could build just one more as a personal favor. The carpenter said yes, but in time it was easy to see that his heart was not in his work. He resorted to shoddy workmanship and used inferior materials. It was an unfortunate way to end his career.

On his last day of work, the contractor, as a gesture of appreciation, gave the carpenter this home for him to live in. How ironic is this? Had he known he was building his own house, he would have done it all so differently. Now he had to live in the home he had built none too well. So it is with us. We build our lives in a distracted way, reacting rather than acting, willing to put out less than the best. Then with a shock we look at the situation we have created and find that we are now living in the very house we have built. Had we realized this, we would have done it differently.

Geometrically, the shortest distance between two points is a straight line. To be able to get from point A to point B quickly can sometimes be beneficial. But if you live your life that way, it won't be as fulfilling because you have been deprived of the struggles—the "real lessons."

So if you are a parent, a coach, a manager, or are leading anybody, make sure things are not too easy. Because life is not easy, and you want to prepare those you are leading for the valleys of life. The ultimate measure of your character isn't the peaks you reach but, the valleys from which you emerge.

Life Never Goes in a Straight Line

Today we see adults being ultra critical of the way teenagers are acting. We listen to high school coaches talk about their inabilities to get enough players to even fill a team. We hear employers rant and rave about the laziness and poor ethics of the youth. Yet who is to blame? What generation has made things so easy materially for today's youth; there isn't the internal drive or desire to dig down deep and persevere through the turbulence of life?

> There is a close correlation between getting up in the morning and getting up in the world.

In a service industry if your clients get too easy to please, service gets sloppy. And the same applies to your life. If your leaders get too easy, then your efforts often get sloppy. There is no satisfaction in achieving or understanding something that is easy. I am not saying that you want leaders who are tyrants. They must be fair. But for your benefit, they should also be challenging enough to get you to new heights, physically, emotionally, and mentally. One of the best lessons you can learn is to deal with the way the world is, not with the way you wish it was. This is how you develop character.

When people go through tough times, there is an increased level of self-confidence and self-belief. Many shipwrecked lives have become sea worthy only after capsizing a number of times. And this is so very important as we get older because straight lines in our life are fewer each year. But that is OK if you are prepared, if you have mastered the D-A-S-H of the struggle.

> Birds sing after a storm. Why shouldn't we?

Never Forget to Look Up

A man went to steal corn from his neighbor's field. He took his little boy with him to keep a lookout, so as to give warning in case anyone should come along. Before commencing he looked all around, first one way and then the other. Not seeing anyone, he was just about to fill his bag, when his son cried out, "Daddy, there is one way you haven't looked yet!"

The father supposed that someone was coming and asked his son which way he meant. He answered, "You forgot to look up!" The dad, conscience-stricken, took his boy by the hand and hurried home without the corn that he had planned to take.

"In a 1998 Gallop Poll, 80% of Americans said they wanted to experience spiritual growth, up from 50% in 1994."

Without a conscience or someone to look up to, our life will be forever in turmoil. With a conscience, your consciousness will expand. Without a conscience you will become desensitized.

A classic example of this is pointed out in Gail Eisnitz's investigative report of slaughterhouses. In interviewing the "stickers," those who cut the animal open to drain the blood, they all talked about how they had become almost totally desensitized to life. And this spills over into their personal lives. Almost all stickers have been arrested for assault. They beat their spouses, their children, and their friends. Almost all drink heavily, saying that they have no other way of dealing with killing live kicking animals all day long. They all talk about developing an attitude that lets them kill things without any care at all. They flushed their respect for life down the toilet.

> We should listen not merely with our ears but with our heart.

And in a more subtle way, the person carving the Thanksgiving turkey has also become desensitized. Their mouth is watering as they slice through the turkey's muscles, totally oblivious to the suffering of that creature a few weeks or months earlier.

Most of us go through our life as complete strangers to ourselves. It is principally due to our unending race to satisfy ourselves. The government has built a sophisticated interstate highway system, and we can go coast to coast without seeing anything. In many ways we have built a highway of sense gratification that is so self-focused and selfish we don't stop to pay respect to the creator, and at the same time elevating our consciousness.

"Feed your faith and your doubt will starve to death."

I know that there are some of you who have little or no belief that we have a creator and believe that this world just happened by chance. But I also know that when you put on your common sense cap, you will gradually realize that not even a table happens by chance, let alone something as magnificent and complex as your eye. Besides, a big step toward elevating our consciousness is having faith and being humble.

Never Forget to Look Up

Whenever I talk to children, I always ask them if they know what the purpose of children is. Most answer, "To have fun, to enjoy, to be happy." I then answer that the purpose of children is to take care of your parents. Then they giggle. But that has been the purpose until just the most recent generation. Parents have now given their children a consciousness that makes them believe they are the center of the carnival.

Just as little kids by stature have to look up to their parents, so must we, as adults, look up to a higher being.

If you take time to elevate your consciousness, you will be amazed at how much more harmonious your life will be. And when there is more harmony, whether it be emotional, physiological, or mental, you are well on your way to mastering your D-A-S-H.

Why is it that the age-old practice of meditation is flooding the western world now? It is very simple. People inherently know that their lives are full of disharmony. When they wake up in the morning, their body often aches and is in discomfort, and when they go to bed, their brain is still on a runaway treadmill.

Meditation allows you to attempt to introduce some semblance of tranquility into your raceway of life. It affords you an opportunity to get above your ultra-active mind and build a spiritual connection.

Prayer is more prevalent in the western world, but it has been misused. Parents tend to think that it is cute when little Johnny says in his prayers, "God, please get me that red bicycle I saw at Wal-Mart today." Listen to your own prayers. Are they all so full of personal requests?

Never Forget to Look Up

Has God become a doormat for your wants and needs? Or are you elevating your consciousness and your connection with Him by simply appreciating what He has given and offering Him your service.

A parent doesn't appreciate their child always asking for something every time they enter a store. So why would you think you are pleasing your Creator by constantly putting in new requests for things for you.

As mentioned earlier, it is an interesting phenomenon that the more successful people are materially and financially, the less spiritual they usually become. It is as if the illusory state of things and money leads them to the belief that they are now independent. This leads to individuals who, all their life, look outside for what is missing inside. Instead of being unbelievably grateful for having as much as we do, we often forget to acknowledge where we got it from. Before you get out of bed each day, make sure your spiritual compass is working. Design your day so that important things are not forgotten.

Having a consciousness of eternal gratefulness is essential to mastering your D-A-S-H. Just as a parent looks forward to the day when their child says "Thank you" with their heart, so our Creator looks forward to the day when we have enough humility and enough appreciation to want to be of service to Him. With our consciousness on that channel, our D-A-S-H is complete.

> When you were born, you were crying and everyone around you was smiling. Live your life so when you die, you are the one who is smiling and everyone around you is crying.

> I have one life and one chance to make it count

Never Forget to Look Up

for something...I am free to choose what that something is, and the something that I have chosen is my faith. Now, my faith goes beyond theology and religion and requires considerable work and effort. My faith demands—this is not optional—my faith demands that I do whatever I can, wherever I am, whenever I can, for as long as I can with whatever I have to try to make a difference. — Jimmy Carter

Torchlight Publishing recognizes that maintaining a sustainable ecosystem is vital to our planet's future. We support the replanting of trees by donating money to the Global Releaf campaign of American Forests for the replanting of two trees for every tree we use in the production of our books and other materials. American Forests has planted tens of millions of trees in hundreds of ecosystem restoration projects throughout the United States and around the world.

We encourage our readers to support this important program. You can make a tangible difference that will help to improve the environment for generations to come. For more information, please visit their website at: www.globalreleaf.com

PETER BURWASH

LIFE ENRICHMENT LIBRARY

If you liked this book by Peter Burwash you may be interested in the others in his Life Enrichment Library. Please take a look at Peter's four other titles on the following pages and use the ordering information at the back of the book to purchase further copies.

Special prices are available for bulk orders.

By Peter Burwash
Foreword by John Robbins
$9.95 ISBN 978-0-9779785-3-3
4.75" × 6.5", paperback, 256 pgs.

"Read *Total Health* and heed its wise and compassionate counsel, and you will be well on the way to new levels of aliveness, healing, and joy."

— John Robbins, author,
Diet for a New America

Total Health is a wonderful gift for friends, loved ones, or yourself. Order your copy today!

See back page for ordering information

A Simple Guide for Taking Control of Your Health and Happiness Now!

Exploding the Myths of America's Diet and Exercise Programs

Most of us put health and vitality at the top of our goal lists. But we have a hard time achieving it. Despite having so much information at our fingertips and the presence of enormous nutrition, diet, and exercise industries enticing us with promises, most of us find remaining committed to a healthy lifestyle a losing battle. Why?

For more than twenty years Peter Burwash has been answering this question and teaching people around the world the simple truths of how to finally reach their goals of health and happiness. He explains with simplicity and compassion how our food and lifestyle choices have a life-changing impact not only on our own future, health, and happiness, but that of the entire planet.

Dear Teenager

NAVIGATING THE TURBULANT YEARS AND BUILDING A FOUNDATION FOR A MEANINGFUL LIFE

By Peter Burwash

Today's teenagers face an alarming array of hurdles, temptations, and confusing signals. After spending thousands of hours listening to teenagers, Peter Burwash, in a straightforward yet sympathetic style, hones in on their major problems and concerns and offers the knowledge of his own life experiences to help teens through this difficult transitional period. Helpful to parents and mentors of teenagers as well, *Dear Teenager* is a guide to growing up healthy and whole physically, mentally, and spiritually.

A few of Peter Burwash's surefire tips for teens:

"When you get up in the morning, you really only have one major decision to make, and that is whether you are going to have a good attitude or a bad attitude."

"We tend to become the type of person with whom we associate. Do your utmost to choose your friends wisely."

"Most adults look back on their teenage years and say, 'I wish I had known then what I know now'. Why? Because knowledge eliminates fear. And during our years as teenagers, there's so much anxiety and fear that some extra knowledge could go a long way to help paddle through the waves of insecurity."

"Adversity and struggle are such wonderful teachers. Adversity often introduces us to ourselves, and struggle makes us appreciate the end result so much more."

Paperback 4.75 x 6.5 inches, 240 pages, $9.95
ISBN 13: 978-09779785-2-6
See back page for ordering information

How You Can Become a Great Leader

The President of the United States, the Chief Executive of a Fortune 500 company, and the mother of an eight year old Cub Scout are each in a position of leadership. But how do you develop those special qualities that bring success as a leader?

The Key shows clearly and simply the underlying principles that make for successful leadership.

Whether you're Chairman of the Board or a mother of three, in *The Key* you will find a wealth of information to enrich your life.

"Inspirational and compelling bite-size quotes illustrated by motivational stories in two key competitive advantages of the future —service and leadership."
— Dr. Steven Covey, chairman of Covey leadership center and author of *The Seven Habits of Highly Effective People*.

"Peter's firm is the biggest and best of its kind in the world because he follows the precepts outlined in *The Key*. He knows how to create a high-trust culture and a high-energy work force, and he tells you concisely and clearly, from experience, how it's done."
—From the foreword by Isadore Sharp, founder and chairman of Four Seasons hotels and resorts

Paperback 4.75 x 6.5 inches, 240 pages, $9.95
ISBN 13: 978-09779785-0-5
See back page for ordering information

Take charge of your life!

"A blend of practical wisdom and a depth of experience to teach us how to take charge of every aspect of our lives."
—from the foreword by Lee Iacocca

Improving the Landscape of Your Life offers a fresh, practical approach to achieving new levels of personal effectiveness.

Peter Burwash reveals twelve essential habits for succeeding and understanding true happiness.

The happiest people are those who try to help others and who don't necessarily have the best of everything, but they make the best of everything they have.

Although Peter's book is presented in bite-size chapters, don't let this fool you. Inside you'll find twelve very powerful and practical lessons on how to take charge of every aspect of your life.

Paperback 4.75 x 6.5 inches, 144 pages, $9.95
ISBN 13: 978-09779785-1-9

See back page for ordering information

ORDER FORM
CALL & ORDER NOW!

❖ **Telephone orders:** Call 1-888-TORCHLT (1-888-867-2458)

   Have your VISA or MasterCard ready

❖ **Fax orders:** (559)-337-2354

❖ **Postal orders:** PO Box 52, Badger CA 93603

❖ **Web orders:** www.torchlight.com

Please send the following. I understand I may return any books for a full refund—for any reason, no questions asked.

❑ *The Key to Great Leadership* $9.95.....................No. of copies _____
❑ *Total Health* $9.95..No. of copies _____
❑ *Dear Teenager* $9.95...No. of copies _____
❑ *Improving the Landscape of Your Life* $9.95......No. of copies _____
❑ *Master of the DASH* $9.95.................................No. of copies _____

Please add my name to your mailing list so I may receive information on future books published by Torchlight.

Company _____

Name _____

City _____ State _____ Zip _____

Country _____ Phone _____

Sales tax: California residents add 8.25%
Shipping and handling: Book rate: USA and Canada $2.00 for first book and $1.50 for each additional book. Foreign countries $2.50 for first book, $2.00 for each additional book. (Surface shipping may take 3-4 weeks. Foreign orders please allow 6-8 weeks for delivery) Priority Air Mail (USA only) $3.50 per book.

Payment: ❑ Check/money order enclosed ❑ Credit card
   ❑ VISA ❑ MasterCard

Card #_____ Exp.date _____

Name on card_____

Signature _____